Pebble® Plus

Animal Offspring

Cows and Their Calves

Revised Edition

by Margaret Hall

CAPSTONE PRESS
a capstone imprint

Pebble Plus is published by Capstone Press,
1710 Roe Crest Drive,
North Mankato, Minnesota 56003
www.capstonepub.com

Library of Congress Cataloging-in-Publication Data
Names: Hall, Margaret, 1947- author.
Title: Cows and their calves : a 4D book / by Margaret
Hall.
Description: Revised edition. | North Mankato,
Minnesota : Capstone Press, a Capstone imprint,
[2018] | Series: Pebble plus. Animal offspring |
Audience: Ages 4-8. | Includes bibliographical
references and index.
Identifiers: LCCN 2017037869 (print) | LCCN
2017052292 (ebook) | ISBN 9781543508611 (eBook
PDF) | ISBN 9781543508215 (hardback) | ISBN
9781543508338 (pbk.)
Subjects: LCSH: Calves—Juvenile literature. | Cows—
Juvenile literature.
Classification: LCC SF205 (ebook) | LCC SF205 .H26
2018 (print) | DDC 636.2/07—dc23
LC record available at https://lccn.loc.gov/2017037869

Editorial Credits
Gina Kammer, editor; Sarah Bennett, designer;
Morgan Walters, media researcher;
Katy LaVigne, production specialist

Photo Credits
Shutterstock: alberto clemares exposito, 19, arogant,
right 20, Barsan ATTILA, 13, Ewelina Wachala, right
21, GLF Media, 5, Ilia Krivoruk, 9, ivan jimenez foto,
7, jennyt, Cover, jungdosoon, 3, Lakeview Images,
11, MRAORAOR, 15, napocska, left 20, Nicole
Kwiatkowski, 17, Rosa Jay, left 21

Note to Parents and Teachers

The Animal Offspring set supports national science
standards related to life sciences. This book describes
and illustrates cows and their calves. The images
support early readers in understanding the text.
The repetition of words and phrases helps early
readers learn new words. This book also introduces
early readers to subject-specific vocabulary words,
which are defined in the Glossary section. Early
readers may need assistance to read some words and
to use the Table of Contents, Glossary, Read More,
Internet Sites, Critical Thinking Questions, and Index
sections of the book.

Printed in the United States   5914

Table of Contents

Cows

Cows are mammals.

Cows have black, brown,

white, or red hair.

Young cows are

called calves.

Cows and calves graze in pastures on farms and ranches. Cows and calves sometimes live in barns.

A male is a bull.

A female is a cow.

Bulls and cows mate.

A calf begins to grow

inside the cow.

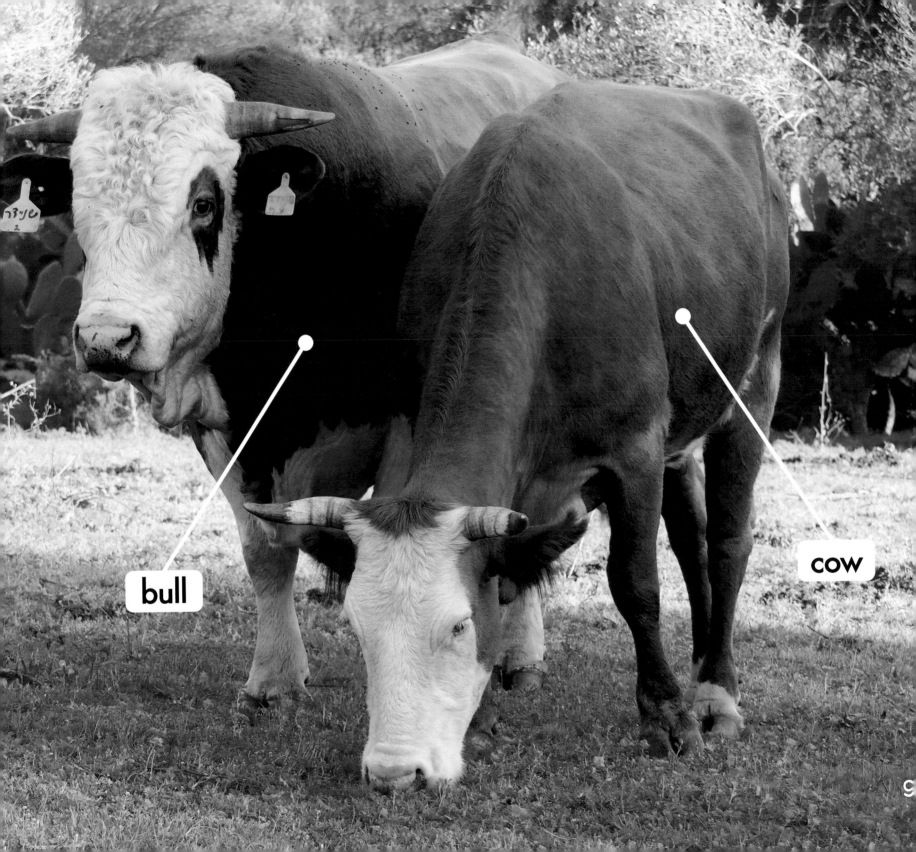

bull

cow

The Calf

The cow gives birth

to a calf.

The cow takes care

of the calf.

Calves have long legs.

Calves can stand up about one hour after they are born.

Calves drink milk

from their mothers.

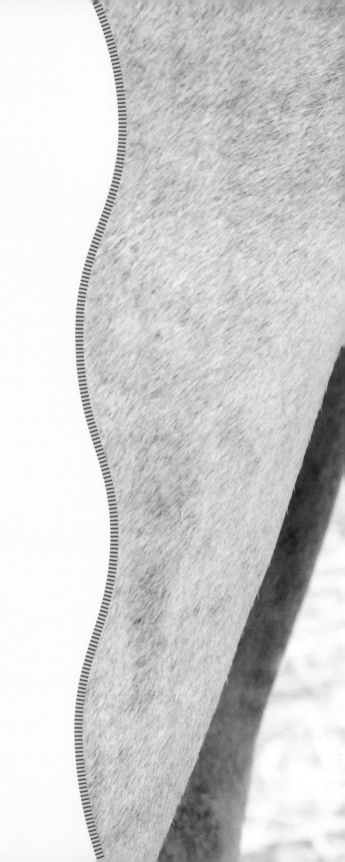

Growing Up

Calves start to eat
hay, grass, and grain
after about one month.

Calves become adults

after about two years.

Watch Cows Grow

birth

adult after
about two years

21

Glossary

birth—the event of being born; cows usually give birth to one calf at a time; cows sometimes have twins

bull—an adult male of the cattle family; bulls can father young; male calves that do not become fathers are called steers

cow—an adult female of the cattle family; a young cow is called a heifer before she gives birth to a calf for the first time

graze—to eat grass and other plants that are growing in a pasture or field

mammal—a warm-blooded animal that has a backbone and hair or fur; female mammals feed milk to their young

mate—to join together to produce young; cows give birth nine months after mating

pasture—land that animals use to graze

Read More

Gibbs, Maddie. *Cows.* New York: PowerKids Press, 2015.

Hughes, Catherine D. *Farm Animals.* Washington, D.C.:
National Geographic, 2016.

Mayerling, Tim. *Calves.* Minneapolis: Jump! Inc., 2017.

Silverman, Buffy. *Meet a Baby Cow.* Minneapolis:
Lerner Publications, 2017.

Internet Sites

Use FactHound to find Internet sites related to this book.

Visit *www.facthound.com*

Just type **9781543508215** and go.

 Check out projects, games and lots more at
www.capstonekids.com

Critical Thinking Questions

1. What things can a calf do soon after it is born?

2. Cows and calves graze in pastures. What does "graze" mean?

3. How does a cow take care of her calf?

Index